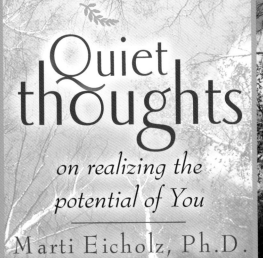

Quiet thoughts

on realizing the potential of You

Marti Eicholz, Ph.D.

Quiet Thoughts on Realizing the Potential of You

To access further resources and learning programs,
please visit www.transformation.org or contact:
Institute for Transformation LLC
550 Kirkland Way, Suite 405, Kirkland, WA 98033
telephone: 425-739-6025 • fax 425-739-0022 • toll-free 888-942-9777
e-mail institute@transformation.org

Library of Congress Catalog Card Number: 99-095083

FIRST EDITION

ISBN 0-9653100-6-X

Contents

Introduction

Would you like to live a more empowered life,
full of joy and energy?
Are you ready to discover more
of your innate potential?
Do you feel like it's finally time to become the
person you were born to be?
Then turn within, and embark on
a journey of self-awareness.
Inside you is a dynamic, inspired person, just waiting
to be nurtured and released.

All that's required is your desire and your willingness to consider new ideas. All you have to do is relax and allow new goodness to flow into your life.

Begin by nurturing your soul, mind, body, and spirit.

Your personal style might be to walk in the woods, to relax at the beach, or simply to enjoy a moment of solitude in your own home.

Listen to your inner self.

Then take care of that wonderful inner you, in ways that are both meaningful and satisfying.

Nurturing yourself is the very best thing you can do for those you love.

You see, when we find our own lives exhilarating, we can offer greater service to others.

We have the desire and the energy to encourage, strengthen, and nourish those around us.

We spread joy without even trying.

It's in the air when we walk into a room. It's in the sparkle of our smile. It's in the dance of our step.

The best news is that the springs of inspiration are inside of you right NOW. And when you dwell on inspiring thoughts, you tap into your OWN wisdom.

Let ideas abide gently in your mind. Give positive thoughts ample room for consideration—and allow new dimensions of harmony and happiness to fill your heart.

Dedicated ...
to those of you who are willing to look
inside themselves for answers.

Special Recognition
to
Alesa Lightbourne, Ph.D.
and
Michelle Bartanen

Self-Esteem

Everything starts with liking yourself.
Everything!
Self-esteem is simply a measure
of how much we value ourselves.
And this is totally up to us.
Nobody forces you to put yourself down.
Nobody makes you think that you're unworthy,
or ugly, or deficient in any way.
These are all things that we do
TO OURSELVES.

While it's true that many of our internal "tapes"
come from childhood, we always have
the power to change these tapes.

When you clearly voice your beliefs,
you reveal who you really are.
Have the courage to speak your mind,
and express your real self.
This is how you prove that
you're someone who matters
and who is worthy of respect.

Only when you understand and like yourself
can you turn outward to those around you,
and say with confidence, "I have this to share."

Your self-esteem is built on accomplishment.
When you put forth some effort,
you have something to be proud of.
Even failures count as accomplishments.
They're proof that you tried, and you did your best.
Viewed in this manner,
ANY type of accomplishment helps build
self-esteem, regardless of the outcome.

People generally accept you at your own evaluation.

Act like nobody, and you'll get ignored.

Act important, and people will treat you like a VIP.

Discipline yourself to be dependable.

Meet challenges head-on.

Face difficulties with courage.

Choose to be strong, rather than weak.

Your self-confidence will increase dramatically!

Recognize that you are the author of your choices,
actions, and emotions.
You write the script of your life.
This means that YOU
are responsible for your successes.
And no one else can make you happy
or give you self-esteem.

Begin to think of yourself as a valuable resource
with energy and ideas to contribute
and you can't help but make a positive difference
in the world around you.

Self-esteem is a dynamic source of energy.
It empowers and motivates you, and makes it
possible for you to attain your dreams.
It also has a direct impact
on your values and goals,
the way you perceive the world,
and the way you react to situations
and meet challenges.
That's why self-esteem
is such an important starting point
on the journey to self-awareness.

How do you build up your inner reserves
of self-esteem?
First, discover who you are.
Do this with all dimensions of your being:
the physical, mental, emotional, and spiritual YOU.
Understand and validate your feelings and desires.
Accept yourself, as you are,
right this very moment.

Self-esteem is the immune system
of your consciousness.
It protects you from negativity.
It gives you the psychological strength
to overcome difficulties.
It makes you resilient in the face of adversity,
so you are better able to achieve your goals.

Love

Self-awareness is really all about love.
To love and be loved are the
greatest joys in the world.
Almost all of us wish we had MORE
of this precious commodity.
Would you like to find a way to make certain
you ALWAYS have the love
you want and need?

Take care of yourself first.
Only then will you have enough love in your heart
to give to everyone and everything
that enters your sphere of influence.

Love means being gentle and tender
in your approach to all things.
Love yourself, and love your work,
so you radiate enthusiasm and actually help
transform the world.

Love can also be described as passion—
passion for living, passion for life.
Be open to the possibilities of passion.
Look for it in even the most mundane
activities during your day.
Adopt a passionate attitude toward working,
gardening, exercising, driving,
cooking, playing, and parenting and
display your passion in all types of relationships.
It will give you a new vitality, and provide
the excitement that we all seek in our lives today.

But most of all, love means caring.
Caring is the gift of attention.
Give the gift of attention—positive attention—
to the people, creatures, and even objects
around you.
Do you want to be cared FOR?
Then extend a caring attitude to everyone
and everything.

Self-Image

Self-image is the way we view ourselves
from the inside out.
It's the way we evaluate ourselves
in comparison with other people.
It's the measurement
of whether we feel "okay" about ourselves.

The good news about self-image is that
it's entirely in your own hands.
No one on the face of this earth
can make you feel inferior
without your permission.

Self-image is many factors, all rolled into one.
Knowledge, intention, commitment,
physical condition, and emotional satisfaction
all contribute to self-image
and enhance our sense of well being.

One secret for strengthening
your self-image is to "act as if."
Act like the healthy, open, and confident person
you want to be.
Don't think of this as pretending.
Think of it as PRACTICING!

If you like yourself and think you're terrific,
most people around you will agree.
One condition, however,
is that you believe that others are terrific, too.
A positive self-image
is the polar opposite of arrogance.
A positive self-image values others
at the same time that it values self.

Everything starts with liking yourself.

Keep your best self-image in the front of your mind.
Revisit this shining self-image often
throughout your day.
Remember that you make
or break yourself by your self-image.

Energy

True inspirational energy
comes from learning who we are,
and then BEING who we are.

The goal is to create a free flow of energy
throughout each day so that we draw in
positive energy, and we generously expend energy
through creative and loving actions.

Judgment and controlling actions
stop up the free flow of energy.
When you're critical of another person,
you give away some of your energy,
and you feel depleted.

On the other hand, when you go with the flow,
you access an ever-present source of new power.

Raw energy comes to us
from good food and fresh air.
Remember to eat right and get outside
to ensure a good source of energy.

When you appreciate the beauty and uniqueness
of things, you RECEIVE energy.
The more you are able to love and appreciate others,
the more energy you draw to yourself.
This energy accumulates,
leading to healing and growth.
Then when you get to a level where you feel love,
you can give energy back.

You are a unique being,
surrounded by a world of energy.
You can consciously project your energy.
You do this in every activity.
You also do this when you are tolerant, kind,
understanding, and flexible.
ASK for these attributes and watch them
manifest in your life.

Sometimes we project our energy in self-sacrifice.
If done in a spirit of respect for both others
and ourselves, this can be very enriching.
But when we overdo it,
and give too much without taking care of ourselves,
we end up feeling drained.
Take care of your own needs,
along with those of others,
so you will overflow with positive energy.

Growth

Try something new every single day.
Eagerly accept opportunities
to learn and grow.
Seek out people and situations that
challenge your comfort level.
Like a bud in spring, look for new ways
to stretch toward the sun.

When difficulties arise,
don't let them make you bitter.
Instead, use them to make you better.

Growth requires that you look
for alternatives in your life.
The pattern that you are currently in
is only one of thousands of possibilities.
Broaden your mental horizons.
Ask yourself whether there may be
better alternatives in your physical, mental,
emotional, and spiritual realms.

Look back only to learn.
Yes, it is important to understand
your early influences.
But it's even more important to move beyond
the past, to deal with your present,
and to shape your future.

Take charge of your life.
Decide which labor pains you are willing to
experience, in order to give birth
to your highest self.

The quest for growth is unending.
We continue to add to, reshape, and reform
our identities throughout our lives.
This is what keeps us young inside
and full of zest for life.

You can learn from others' experiences.
But often the only way we can learn lessons at a
deep level is to go through them ourselves.
Be aware of this when people try to give you advice.
Claim your growth opportunities for yourself!

Creating a new vision for yourself may require
overcoming or modifying powerful programming
that occurred during childhood.
Often reprogramming childhood messages results in
extraordinary healing.

In the ongoing process of becoming who you are,
develop the habit of viewing each
and every obstacle as a precious opportunity
to learn and grow.

Success

In your own hands,
you hold two types of seeds—the seeds of failure
and the seeds for true greatness.

If you have experienced failure in the past,
consider that failure a state of mind.
Often failure is merely a disguise for another word
that begins with "F" – feedback.
Failure can give us the feedback we need
to try again—and to succeed.

To be successful, you have to be ready to give
100 percent.
Fortunately, that's exactly what you have to give—
to any project, endeavor, or relationship.

The first step lies in realizing that your success—
and your happiness—start with YOU.

Make a victory list to remind you
of all your past successes.
Then look at it regularly, especially when
you're tempted to start feeling discouraged.
Realize how much you really HAVE accomplished.
And give yourself a big pat on the back
for a job well done.

A wise approach for effectiveness and success
is to learn your own style.
Become familiar with the things
that FEEL right for you—
the things that make you comfortable,
that come easy to you.
Accept this style, and be thankful for it.
From there, you can adapt to
the other styles around you.
And you'll know that you're being true to yourself.

Success is something we can teach children.
We typically tell children what they SHOULD do.
Instead, we have to help children
discover what they CAN do.
Then we can show them
how to make their dreams reality.

The one quality that all successful people have,
no matter what their fields of endeavor,
is PERSISTENCE.
Winners know how to stick with a project,
despite seeming setbacks and temporary failures.
Look at the winners around you
and see how they stand head and shoulders
above everyone else for their extraordinary ability to
NEVER TO GIVE UP.

Success also depends on a combination
of capabilities. You hear and forget.
You hear, and you remember.
When you see, hear, and remember,
you understand—and then you succeed!

Think of success as being a journey,
not a destination. This will encourage
lifelong learning and growth.

The most important step
in reaching your objectives is the first step.
If you never start moving,
it's certain that you'll never arrive.

Wisdom

You may inherit wealth, but never wisdom.
Wisdom comes from a lifelong process
of discovering who you really are.

Anger has great power—destructive power.
It can even be fatal.
The best advice is to look for ways
to replace anger with kindness.
Become known for your kind and loving heart.

Real security comes from knowing
you can handle yourself graciously,
no matter what happens.

Inner strength requires time alone.
Are you investing the time you need
to tend your inner garden?

Never ignore your own feelings.
Your emotions are gifts from your unconscious.
Value and validate them,
even when they feel uncomfortable or unpleasant.

It's a lot easier to react than to think.
What reactions are you ready to convert
into positive thoughts?

Leave spaces in every day
to do something spontaneous—
for you AND for someone else.

No one who lightens another's burden
is useless in this world.

Of all the diseases known to man,
conceit is the oddest.
It makes everyone sick
except the person afflicted with it.

Be generous with praise.

Don't be hard on yourself.
Instead, just work hard.

The better things go today,
the more chances you have for pleasure
and harmony tomorrow.

Kindness is more important than perfection.
That's because kind words and deeds are eternal.
Their positive impacts will last forever.

There are three things
no one can ever take away from you:
your education, your experience,
and your memories.
Invest your life energy in these timeless treasures.

Travel light.
Jettison your pride, fear, and inflexibility.
Instead, carry with you only knowledge,
power, and wisdom.
These will never weigh you down.

Let go of envy, too.
It's the enemy of your happiness and peace of mind.

Power

Your resources—namely your time,
skills, and energy —form the basis of
your personal power.
You can marshal these resources and begin living
a fuller life, right now.
Take control over the things you can change.
Maximize your positives.
Minimize your negatives.
Find new ways to express the real, dynamic YOU.

Believe in your power to rise above adversity,
and the necessary strength
will be given to you.

If you want the circumstances in your life to change,
take action.
Right now, you have the power
to turn things around, improve relationships,
enhance your health,
and live a life of increased potential.

To increase your personal power,
reward yourself each time you complete
an exercise in self-growth.
Don't evaluate whether your efforts
resulted in success or failure.
Praise yourself for stepping outside
of your comfort zone, and for daring to
try new things.

If you don't like what you see
when you look at who you really are,
remember that you
ALWAYS have the power of choice.
You decide what you will think and
what actions you will take.

Never forget the enormous responsibility
that personal power entails.
No longer can you whine, whimper, or complain
about the rotten hand that fate deals you.
You are the one accepting the cards.
You are the one who chooses how to play.

To build up your personal power reserves,
spend time with people who are positive,
like you are.
Make friends with people who encourage you
in your dreams.
Stay away from the naysayers and the critics,
the pessimists and the so-called realists.
Choose relationships with people whose spirits soar.

Believe in what you're doing.
Convey your commitment to others.
You can turn their doubts into admiration,
and claim additional power for yourself
at the same time.

Take a small step toward
what you really want in life.
See how liberating this one step can be!

You

YOU—are the chief executive officer
of your own life.
You are nothing less than a co-creator
with the universe.
You choose what to believe.
And based on these choices, you create
the experiences of your life.

You cannot affirm the dignity and greatness
in others until you recognize
these aspects of yourself.

Make the extra effort to treat yourself well.
If you do, you'll find that you are better able to
experience your own depth, and then to share the
finest parts of yourself with others.

What happens to you is not as important as
how you react to the things that happen.

Your mind completes whatever picture
you put into it.
So think carefully about the mental images
you decide to hold.
What you are thinking about becoming
is actually what you ARE becoming.

Challenges come when you least expect them.
Prepare yourself in advance
with strong inner resources.

Your level of maturity is nothing more
(and nothing less) than a measure
of how well you handle life's ups and downs.

There's only one person
that will be there for you 24 hours a day—
and that's YOU.

One of the paradoxes in life
is that we MUST nurture ourselves
and give ourselves good, kind, and loving messages.
But we must also avoid
staying focused on ourselves.
If we think only about ourselves, we're guaranteed
to be miserable.

Listen to your inner voice.
Negative thoughts and perceptions
are messages from your inner self.
They need to be heard, and then answered.

Your own intuition is
an invaluable (and valid) source of information.
Turn to it often for guidance.
Trust both the warnings and the serendipities
it provides.

Stress doesn't "happen" to you.
Stress is generated in your own mind.
It is your reaction to the things that occur—
and only you can control
how these things will affect you.

Be mindful of your fantasies.
Collect them, treasure them, and do everything
you can to act on them.
Your fantasies can tell you how you really wish to
express yourself.

Above all, tend to yourself
as you would to a beloved garden—
with the utmost tenderness, respect, and passion.

Relationships

Seek happiness
in the warmth of your friendships.

Living in harmony with another person is an art.
It requires paying attention
to many details, one at a time, over and over,
day after day.
The goal is consistently to give your partner
your very best.

To make a relationship work,
live each day as if it were the only one the two of you
will ever have together.

Whether you're talking, listening, or being silent
with your partner, savor the moment.

Never take another person for granted.
Show your partner only kindness
and understanding.
Express your pride in your partner, both privately
and with close friends.

The most important ingredient in any relationship
is mutual respect.

Although it's natural
to fall into patterns when you live with someone,
try to make each day full of variety and adventure.
Celebrate small delights.
Relish everyday joys and intimacies.
Look for every opportunity to create
magical moments to enrich your time together.

Become a keen observer of the silent signals
your partner sends you.
Then be emotionally available to discuss
issues of all kinds.

Schedule private time with your partner
on a regular basis.
Relax together, and be truly attentive.
Express appreciation for the qualities you love most
in each other.

Be silent with your partner, too, sometimes.
Special time spent in silence is sometimes
more healing than hours of discussion.

Closing

*Now you know where to go to find inner peace,
confidence, and personal power.*
You go within and tap the rich inner resources
you find there.
It's somewhere you can go day or night,
regardless of the circumstances you find yourself in.
It's a place that nobody can
take away from you, nobody can destroy, and
nobody can close down.

In fact, it's a place where
you are the master of your own fate.
YOU can control your destiny
by making better choices,
selecting nurturing thoughts, and opening
yourself to new possibilities.
Proceed along this path, knowing that you
will discover many treasures
along your way and that you will be led safely back,
again, with a greater understanding of yourself.
Take your time and enjoy your journey.